Spring Spreads to "Nutty" Breads

by Marilyn LaPenta

Consultant:
Mandi Pek, MS, RD, CSP, CDN

BEARPORT PUBLISHING

NEW YORK, NEW YORK

Credits

All food illustrations by Kim Jones

Publisher: Kenn Goin
Editor: Joy Bean
Creative Director: Spencer Brinker
Design: Debrah Kaiser

Library of Congress Cataloging-in-Publication Data

La Penta, Marilyn.
  Spring spreads to "nutty" breads / by Marilyn LaPenta.
     pages cm. — (Yummy tummy recipes: seasons)
  Audience: Ages 7-12.
  Includes bibliographical references and index.
  ISBN 978-1-61772-744-3 (library binding) — ISBN 1-61772-744-X (library binding)
  1. Seasonal cooking—Juvenile literature. 2. Spring—Juvenile literature. I. Title.
  TX652.5.L2825 2013
  641.5'64—dc23
                              2012039829

For more information, write to Bearport Publishing Company, Inc., 45 West 21st Street, Suite 3B, New York, New York, 10010. Printed in the United States of America.

10 9 8 7 6 5 4 3 2 1

Contents

Making Healthy Spring Treats

Get ready to make some yummy spring snacks! All the recipes in *Spring Spreads to "Nutty" Breads* make delicious treats. Many of them use fresh fruits and vegetables as part of their ingredients.

In early spring, carrots and other root vegetables along with potatoes and greens, such as asparagus and artichokes, are ready to be picked. Spring also brings strawberries and other fruits. You can find these and other fresh-picked items at your local farmer's market or at a nearby farm. **Produce** that is eaten when it's fresh often has better flavor and nutrition than fruits and vegetables that have been refrigerated for weeks or months and shipped long distances.

The great thing about making your own food with fresh ingredients is that you will avoid the **preservatives** in many **pre-made** foods, which are not always good for the body. For ideas on how to make the recipes in this book even healthier, use the suggestions on page 22.

Getting Started

Use these cooking tips and safety and tool guidelines to make the best spreads and breads you've ever tasted.

Tips

Here are a few tips to get your cooking off to a great start.

- Quickly check out the Prep Time, Cooking Time, Tools, and Servings information at the top of each recipe. It will tell you how long the recipe takes to prepare, the tools you'll need, and the number of people the recipe serves.

- Once you pick a recipe, set out the tools and ingredients that you will need on your worktable.

- Before and after cooking, wash your hands well with warm soapy water to kill any germs.

- Wash fruits and vegetables, as appropriate, to get rid of any dirt and chemicals.

- Put on an apron or smock to protect your clothes.

- Roll up long shirtsleeves to keep them clean.

- Tie back long hair or cover it to keep it out of the food.

- *Very Important:* Keep the adults happy by cleaning up the kitchen when you've finished cooking.

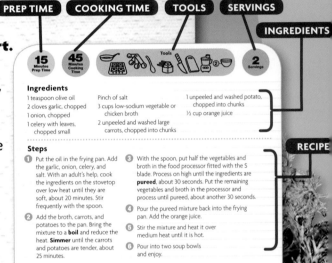

PREP TIME **COOKING TIME** **TOOLS** **SERVINGS**

INGREDIENTS

15 Minutes Prep Time   **45** Minutes Cooking Time   Tools   **2** Servings

Ingredients

1 teaspoon olive oil
2 cloves garlic, chopped
1 onion, chopped
1 celery with leaves, chopped small

Pinch of salt
3 cups low-sodium vegetable or chicken broth
2 unpeeled and washed large carrots, chopped into chunks

1 unpeeled and washed potato, chopped into chunks
½ cup orange juice

RECIPE

Steps

1. Put the oil in the frying pan. Add the garlic, onion, celery, and salt. With an adult's help, cook the ingredients on the stovetop over low heat until they are soft, about 20 minutes. Stir frequently with the spoon.

2. Add the broth, carrots, and potatoes to the pan. Bring the mixture to a **boil** and reduce the heat. **Simmer** until the carrots and potatoes are tender, about 25 minutes.

3. With the spoon, put half the vegetables and broth in the food processor fitted with the S blade. Process on high until the ingredients are **pureed**, about 30 seconds. Put the remaining vegetables and broth in the processor and process until pureed, about another 30 seconds.

4. Pour the pureed mixture back into the frying pan. Add the orange juice.

5. Stir the mixture and heat it over medium heat until it is hot.

6. Pour into two soup bowls and enjoy.

The word carrot comes from the Greek word karoton.

Be Safe

Cook safely by having an adult around to help with these activities:

- Using a sharp knife or peeler
- Using the stove, microwave, blender, food processor, toaster, or other electrical appliances
- Removing hot pans from the oven (Always use pot holders.)
- Frying foods on top of the stove (Keep the heat as low as possible to avoid burns from oil splatter.)

Tools You Need

Here's a guide to the tools you will need to make the various recipes in this book.

 Spoon

 Mixing spoon

 Slotted spoon

 Wooden spoon

 Fork

Knife

Butter knife

 Spatula

 Can opener

 Toothpick

Strainer

Whisk

 Measuring cups

Measuring spoons

Pot holders

 Colander

Cutting board

Soup bowl

Small mixing bowl

Medium mixing bowl

Large mixing bowl

Medium glass, 12 ounces

Large glass, 16 ounces

Small plate

Grater

Small microwave dish

 1-quart plastic freezer bag

Paper towels

Muffin tin

Muffin cups

Steamer pot

Frying pan

Wire rack

Electric mixer

Baking dish

Baking sheet with sides

Cookie sheet

9" x 5" bread pan

Mini bread loaf pan

Griddle

Stovetop

Oven

Blender

Refrigerator

Food processor

7

Healthy Artichoke Spread

5 Minutes Prep Time

30 Minutes Cooking Time

Tools

6 Servings

Health Tip

Artichokes are great for a healthy diet. They are low in fat and **calories** (only 25 per artichoke), but high in **fiber** and **nutrients**.

Ingredients

1 14-ounce can artichoke hearts packed in water

4 ounces **low-fat** mozzarella cheese

3 cloves garlic

⅓ cup Parmesan cheese

⅔ cup plain Greek yogurt

dash of salt

Baked tortilla chips, whole wheat crackers, or bread pieces

Steps

1. **Preheat** the oven to 350°F.

2. With an adult's help, open the can of artichokes with the can opener. Put the colander in the sink and drain the artichokes.

3. With the knife, cut the mozzarella cheese into chunks on the cutting board.

4. Put the artichokes, mozzarella cheese, and garlic in the blender. **Blend** on high for 30 seconds.

5. In a medium baking dish, stir the Parmesan cheese, yogurt, and salt together with the mixing spoon.

6. Scrape the mixture out of the blender into the baking dish with the spoon. Stir the two mixtures together in the pan.

7. Bake for 30 minutes or until the mixture is heated through and lightly browned.

8. Carefully remove the dish from the oven with the pot holders.

9. Serve warm or at room temperature with baked tortilla chips, whole wheat crackers, or bread pieces.

Thanos GREEK YOGURT

An artichoke is actually the flower bud of a thistle plant. If not picked, it grows into a beautiful purple flower.

Baked Tortilla Chips

 5 Minutes Prep Time

15 Minutes Cooking Time

Tools

8 Servings

Ingredients

8 6-inch corn tortillas (or spinach or whole wheat wraps)

1 tablespoon olive oil

1 tablespoon lime juice

Sea salt

Your favorite dip or spread

Steps

1. **Preheat** the oven to 350°F.

2. Stack the tortillas in a pile. With an adult's help, use the knife to cut them into six triangles on the cutting board.

3. Sprinkle the olive oil on the baking sheets. Spread the oil with your fingers to coat the trays.

4. Put each triangle chip in the oil and turn it over to coat both sides.

5. Spread the chips out on the baking sheets so they do not touch. Sprinkle them with the lime juice and salt.

6. Bake the chips until they are golden brown and crispy, about 12 to 15 minutes. Watch closely, as they can burn easily.

7. With the pot holders, remove the trays from the oven and let the chips cool for a few minutes.

8. Put the chips on a paper towel to remove any excess oil. Transfer them to the plate and eat with your favorite dip or spread.

Corn tortillas were first made by the Aztecs of Mesoamerica more than 500 years ago. The word *tortilla* is derived from the Spanish word *torta*, which means "round loaf of bread."

Awesome Asparagus Spread

Tools

3 Servings

Ingredients

Water

2 cups asparagus cut into pieces

1 large tomato

2 teaspoons lemon juice

3 tablespoons chopped onion

½ teaspoon salt

¼ teaspoon pepper

1 clove garlic

¼ cup fresh cilantro

Tortilla chips or cut-up vegetables

Steps

1 Put 1 to 2 inches of water in the steamer pot. Bring to a **boil** on the stovetop. Put the asparagus in the steamer and cover. Reduce the heat and **steam** for 5 minutes. Remove the asparagus from the steamer with the slotted spoon and put it in a colander in the sink. Rinse the asparagus under cold water. Wrap the asparagus in paper towels to remove excess water.

2 With the help of an adult, use the knife to cut the tomato into four pieces on the cutting board.

3 Put the asparagus, lemon juice, onion, salt, pepper, garlic, and cilantro in the food processor. Process for 40 seconds or until smooth. Add the tomato. Process for 10 more seconds, leaving some tomato pieces showing.

4 Hold the strainer over the sink. Pour the spread into the strainer to remove excess water.

5 Put the mixture in a small bowl. Refrigerate for several hours.

6 Serve with tortilla chips or fresh, cut-up vegetables.

Asparagus is part of the lily family along with the onion, garlic, leek, and tulip.

Tasty Tuna Spread

5 Minutes Prep Time

Tools

8 Servings

Ingredients

1 6-ounce can tuna packed in water

¼ cup drained pickle relish

2 teaspoons **diced** onion

3 tablespoons lemon juice

1 tablespoon apple cider vinegar

1 tablespoon light mayonnaise

3 ounces softened light cream cheese

2 tablespoons chopped fresh parsley

¼ teaspoon garlic salt

Whole wheat crackers or toast rounds

Steps

1. Ask an adult to help you open the can of tuna with the can opener. Hold the strainer over the sink. Pour the tuna into the strainer to remove excess water.

2. Put the tuna, relish, and onion in the mixing bowl. Add the lemon juice, vinegar, mayonnaise, cream cheese, parsley, and garlic salt. Use the whisk to **blend** the ingredients together.

3. Spread the mixture on whole wheat crackers or toast rounds with the butter knife.

Families with children are twice as likely to have tuna sandwiches for lunch as families with no children.

11

Peanut Butter Banana Nut Bread

10 Minutes Prep Time

1 Hour Cooking Time

Tools

Makes 1 Loaf

Ingredients

Cooking spray

2 large bananas, peeled (the browner, the sweeter)

⅓ cup nonfat yogurt

⅓ cup creamy peanut butter

3 tablespoons softened butter

2 eggs

¼ cup honey

½ cup brown sugar

2 cups whole wheat flour

¾ teaspoon baking soda

¼ teaspoon salt

½ teaspoon cinnamon

½ cup walnuts

Health Tip

Walnuts are full of **vitamins** and other helpful **nutrients**. Research shows that they can decrease your risk of heart disease and other chronic health conditions.

Steps

1. **Preheat** the oven to 350°F. Coat the bread pan with cooking spray.

2. In a small bowl, **mash** the bananas with the fork.

3. Put the mashed bananas, yogurt, peanut butter, butter, and eggs in the large mixing bowl. Use the electric mixer to **cream** the ingredients. Add the honey and sugar, and use the mixer to **blend** the ingredients.

4. With the spoon, mix the flour, baking soda, salt, and cinnamon in another small bowl.

5. Add the flour mixture to the banana mixture and use the mixer to **beat** the ingredients. Using the spoon, stir in the walnuts.

6. Pour the batter into the greased bread pan. Put the pan in the oven and bake for 1 hour and 10 minutes or until a toothpick inserted in the center comes out clean.

7. Carefully remove the pan from the oven with the pot holders. Let the bread cool in the pan on the wire rack for 10 minutes.

8. Remove the bread from the pan by turning the pan over onto the wire rack. (You may have to loosen the bread from the pan by going around the edge with a dull knife.)

Peanut butter can be used to remove gum from hair.

Whole Wheat Yogurt Pancakes

5 Minutes Prep Time

10 Minutes Cooking Time

Tools

Makes 6 Pancakes

Ingredients

¾ cup whole wheat flour

¼ teaspoon salt

½ teaspoon baking soda

1 egg

¾ cup **low-fat** or nonfat yogurt

1 tablespoon melted butter

½ teaspoon honey

1 tablespoon butter for cooking

Butter, maple syrup, or berry sauce

Health Tip

For pancakes with fewer **calories** and fat, substitute applesauce for the melted butter.

Steps

1. In the medium bowl, mix together the flour, salt, and baking soda with the mixing spoon. Set aside.

2. In the small bowl, **beat** the egg lightly with the fork and add in the yogurt, melted butter, and honey. Mix with the fork.

3. Add the egg mixture to the flour mixture and use the wooden spoon to gently **blend** the ingredients. The batter will be thick.

4. Ask an adult to help you melt the butter in the large frying pan or griddle over medium heat on the stovetop.

5. When a drop of batter bubbles in the pan, that means the pan is hot enough. Use a spoon to drop the batter into the pan making about a 4-inch round pancake. Repeat until the batter is gone.

6. Cook each pancake over medium heat until the edges begin to brown and bubbles appear in the center. The pancake should be golden brown underneath. Lift a corner slightly with the spatula to check the underside.

7. When the underside is brown, flip the pancake over and press once with the spatula. Heat until the other side is lightly browned (peek using the spatula).

8. Remove each pancake from the pan with the spatula and put it on the plate. Serve with butter, maple syrup, or the berry sauce on page 14 of this book.

low-fat yogurt

For more than a thousand years, pancakes have been eaten on Mardi Gras (called Pancake Day in some parts of the world).

Quick-and-Delicious Berry Sauce

Tools

Makes 2 Cups

Health Tip

Use **organic** or sugar-free preserves to make this an even healthier sauce.

Ingredients

12 ounces fresh or thawed frozen strawberries (may use other berries)

½ cup raspberry preserves

1 tablespoon lemon juice

Steps

1. If you are using fresh strawberries, ask an adult to help you use the knife to remove the stems and leaves.

2. Put the strawberries, preserves, and lemon juice in the blender and cover.

3. **Blend** on low for 20 to 30 seconds or until the mixture is **pureed** and completely smooth.

4. Pour the mixture into an airtight container and store in the refrigerator.

5. Serve on pancakes, waffles, yogurt, ice cream, or any dessert.

On average, there are between 150 and 200 seeds on the surface of every strawberry.

organic RASPBERRY PRESERVES

Chocolate Fruit Smoothie

5 Minutes Prep Time

Tools

1 Serving

Ingredients

½ cup strawberries

½ cup chocolate frozen yogurt

½ cup **low-fat** milk

½ frozen banana (or ½ fresh banana, peeled, and 3 ice cubes)

Steps

1. With the help of an adult, use the knife to remove the stem and leaves from the strawberries. Set aside one strawberry for decoration.

2. Put the yogurt, milk, strawberries, and banana in the blender.

3. **Blend** on high for 30 seconds or until the mixture is smooth.

4. Pour the mixture into the tall glass. Put one strawberry on the rim of the glass to decorate.

Eating yogurt has been shown to improve bad breath.

Frozen Chocolate Yogurt

On-the-Go Fruit Frosty

2 Minutes Prep Time

Tools

1 Serving

Ingredients

4 to 6 heaping cups frozen fruit (use your favorites: berries, pineapple, mango, peaches, and bananas are good options)

1 cup juice (Use your favorite: grape, orange, pineapple, cranberry, and apple are good options.)

½ cup water

Steps

1. Put the frozen fruit in the blender.*

2. Pour the juice and water into the blender.

3. **Blend** on high for 30 seconds or until the mixture is smooth (if t is too thick, add more water).

4. Pour into a tall glass and enjoy.

* If you want to freeze your own fruit, ask an adult to help you use the knife to cut your favorite fruits into bite-size pieces on the cutting board. Berries can be left whole. Put the fruit in a freezer bag and store in the freezer for one day before using.

Bananas are actually an herb, not a fruit. They are the world's largest herb and are related to the orchid and lily families.

Carrot Vegetable Soup

15 Minutes Prep Time

45 Minutes Cooking Time

Tools

2 Servings

Ingredients

1 teaspoon olive oil

2 cloves garlic, chopped

1 onion, chopped

1 celery with leaves, chopped small

Pinch of salt

3 cups low-sodium vegetable cr chicken broth

2 unpeeled and washed large carrots, chopped into chunks

1 unpeeled and washed potato, chopped into chunks

½ cup orange juice

Steps

1. Put the oil in the frying pan. Add the garlic, onion, celery, and salt. With an adult's help, cook the ingredients on the stovetop over low heat until they are soft, about 20 minutes. Stir frequently with the spoon.

2. Add the broth, carrots, and potatoes to the pan. Bring the mixture to a **boil** and reduce the heat. **Simmer** until the carrots and potatoes are tender, about 25 minutes. Then turn off the heat and let the vegetables cool for a few minutes.

3. With the spoon, put half the vegetables and broth in the food processor fitted with the S blade. Process on high until the ingredients are **pureed**, about 30 seconds. Put the remaining vegetables and broth in the processor and process until pureed, about another 30 seconds.

4. Pour the pureed mixture back into the frying pan. Add the orange juice.

5. Stir the mixture and heat it over medium heat until it is hot.

6. Pour into two soup bowls and enjoy.

The word carrot comes from the Greek word karoton.

17

Apricot Oatmeal Cookies

15 Minutes Prep Time

12 Minutes Cooking Time

Tools

②

Makes 36 Cookies

Ingredients

Cooking spray
½ cup whole wheat flour
¼ teaspoon salt
¼ teaspoon baking soda

2 cups old-fashioned oats
3 tablespoons softened butter
¼ cup brown sugar
¼ cup honey

2 eggs
½ cup chopped apricots
½ cup shredded coconut

Health Tip

Apricots are an excellent source of vitamin A and **fiber**.

Steps

① **Preheat** the oven to 350°F. Lightly coat the cookie sheets with cooking spray.

② In the small bowl, stir together the flour, salt, baking soda, and oats with the mixing spoon. Set aside.

③ Put the butter, sugar, and honey in the large mixing bowl. Mix the ingredients well with the electric mixer.

④ Crack each egg on the side of the large bowl and let it slide in. Mix thoroughly.

⑤ Add the flour mixture to the butter mixture. Mix the ingredients with the electric mixer until they are well combined and form a dough.

⑥ With the spoon, stir in the apricots and coconut.

⑦ Drop the dough by heaping teaspoons onto the cookie sheets. Bake for 12 to 15 minutes.

⑧ Carefully remove the cookie sheets from the oven with the pot holders. With the spatula, move the cookies to the wire rack to cool.

Note: These cookies are high and rounded. If you like flat cookies, flatten each cookie with the spatula before baking.

Apricots are sometimes called stone fruits, just like nectarines, plums, peaches, and cherries. That is because of the hard pit found in the center of each of these fruits.

Yummy Chocolate Pieces

10 Minutes Prep Time

13 Minutes Cooking Time

Tools

Makes 60 Pieces

Ingredients

12 graham crackers broken into quarters

1 cup unsalted butter

1 cup light brown sugar

1 cup chopped pecans

2 cups semi-sweet chocolate chips

Steps

1. **Preheat** the oven to 350°F.
2. Place the graham crackers closely together on the ungreased cookie sheet.
3. Ask an adult to help you melt the butter in the frying pan on the stovetop over medium heat.
4. Add the brown sugar and stir with the wooden spoon. Bring the ingredients to a **boil**.
5. Boil for 3 minutes while stirring constantly. The ingredients will **caramelize**.
6. Use the pot holders to hold the frying pan as you pour the butter mixture over the graham crackers until they are completely covered.
7. Sprinkle the pecans on top to cover each cracker.
8. Put the crackers in the oven and bake for 10 minutes.
9. Carefully remove the pan from the oven with the pot holders. Sprinkle the chocolate chips to cover the top of each cracker. Let the crackers stand for 1 to 2 minutes. Then spread the melted chocolate chips over the crackers with a dull knife.
10. Let the crackers cool in the pan.
11. When cool, break the crackers apart into pieces. Try putting them in the freezer. They taste great cold.

Hint: Put the whole pan in the refrigerator to cool, and the crackers will break apart more easily.

In 1829 graham crackers were invented by Sylvester Graham as a health food. He believed in using only whole wheat flour sweetened with honey or molasses. He was considered a health nut.

Carrot Muffins

Health Tip

To reduce **calories** and **fat**, you can use ½ cup vegetable oil and ½ cup vanilla yogurt instead of butter.

Ingredients

Cooking spray
½ cup whole wheat flour
½ cup all-purpose flour
½ cup oat bran or quick oatmeal

1 teaspoon baking soda
1 teaspoon cinnamon
2 unpeeled and washed carrots
½ cup softened butter

½ cup brown sugar
2 large bananas, peeled
4 ounces unsweetened applesauce
2 eggs

Steps

1. **Preheat** the oven to 375°F.

2. Coat the muffin tins with cooking spray or use paper muffin cups.

3. In a small bowl, stir together the flours, bran, baking soda, and cinnamon with the mixing spoon.

4. With an adult's help, use the knife to cut off the ends of the carrots on the cutting board and throw them away. **Grate** the carrots using the grater.

5. In the large bowl, **cream** the butter and the brown sugar with the electric mixer.

6. In a small bowl, **mash** the bananas with the fork. Add the bananas, applesauce, and carrots to the butter mixture. Crack each egg on the side of the bowl and let it slide in. Continue mixing these ingredients with the mixer until they are well blended.

7. Add the flour mixture to the large bowl and mix with the butter mixture until it is just combined, forming a thick dough.

8. Spoon the dough into the muffin cups, leaving a ¼-inch space at the top of each cup.

9. Bake until you can insert the toothpick in the center of the muffin and it comes out clean. It takes about 15 to 20 minutes for large muffins to bake and 10 to 12 minutes for mini muffins.

10. Carefully remove the tins with the pot holders and let them cool for 10 minutes on the wire rack.

11. Take the muffins out of the tins and move them to the wire rack to continue cooling. (You may have to run a dull knife around the edges of the muffin cups to loosen each muffin if paper cups were not used.)

Carrots were first grown as medicine, not as food.

Orange Pecan Mini Breads

15 Minutes Prep Time

40 Minutes Cooking Time

Tools

Makes 3 Mini Loaves

Ingredients

- Cooking spray
- 1 cup all-purpose flour, plus some for dusting pans
- 1 cup whole wheat flour
- 1 teaspoon baking powder
- ½ teaspoon salt
- ½ cup softened butter
- ½ cup honey
- ¾ cup sugar
- 2 eggs
- ⅓ cup orange juice
- ½ cup chopped pecans
- 1 tablespoon grated orange **rind**

Steps

1 **Preheat** the oven to 350°F. Coat the mini bread pans with cooking spray. Sprinkle with flour.

2 In the small bowl, mix together the flours, baking powder, and salt with the spoon. Set aside.

3 Put the butter, honey, and sugar in the large mixing bowl. Use the electric mixer to **cream** them together until light and fluffy.

4 Crack each egg on the side of the bowl and let it slide in. **Beat** the eggs well into the butter mixture.

5 Add the flour mixture to the butter mixture and mix well with the electric mixer until dough forms. Add the orange juice, pecans, and orange rind to the dough and **blend** all the ingredients together using the mixer.

6 Pour the dough into the bread pans.

7 Bake until you can insert the toothpick in the center of the bread and it comes out clean, about 35 to 40 minutes.

8 Carefully remove the pans from the oven with the pot holders. Place the pans on the wire rack to cool for 10 minutes.

9 Remove the bread loaves from the pans by turning the pans over onto the wire rack. (First you may have run a dull knife around the edges of the pans to loosen each loaf.) Enjoy.

Rubbing a fresh orange peel on your skin can repel mosquitoes.

Healthy Tips

Always Read Labels

Labels tell how much fat, sugar, **vitamins**, and other **nutrients** are in food. If you compare one bottle of juice with another, for example, you can determine which one has fewer **calories**, less sugar, and so on. Don't forget to look at the serving size when comparing foods.

Make Recipe Substitutions

While all the recipes in this book call for wholesome ingredients, you can make even healthier snacks by substituting some ingredients for others. For example:

- Dairy: use nonfat or **low-fat** instead of full fat dairy products such as yogurt, cheese, and milk. Soy or almond milk can also be used instead of cow's milk. Coconut oil may be substituted for butter.

- Juice: choose 100 percent fruit juice or juice with no added sugar.

- Sugar: use honey, agave, or maple syrup instead of sugar in recipes.

- Fruit: if fresh fruit is unavailable, use freshly frozen unsweetened fruit.

- Flour: use whole wheat flour or a combination of all-purpose flour and whole wheat in baked goods.

Nutrition Facts

Serving Size 1 Container (200g)

Amount Per Serving

Calories 150   Calories from Fat 35

% Daily Value*

Total Fat 4g	6%
Sat. Fat 3g	15%
Trans Fat 0g	
Cholesterol 10mg	0%
Sodium 65mg	3%
Total Carbohydrate 8g	3%
Fiber 0g	3%
Sugars	0%
Protein 20g	
	40%

Vitamin A 2% • Vitamin C 0% • Calcium 20% • Iron 0%

*Percent Daily Values (DV) are based on a 2,000 calorie

Glossary

antioxidants (an-tee-OK-suh-duhnts) substances in certain foods that may prevent cell damage, which can cause disease

beat (BEET) to stir vigorously

blend (BLEND) to mix two or more ingredients together

boil (BOIL) to heat up a liquid until it starts to bubble

calories (KAL-uh-reez) measurements of the amount of energy that food provides

caramelize (CAR-meh-lize) to change a food into caramel

cholesterol (kuh-LESS-tuh-rol) a fatty substance people need to digest food; too much in the blood can increase the chance of heart disease

cream (KREEM) to mix something together until it looks like cream in color and texture

diced (DICED) cut into small cubes

fiber (FYE-bur) a substance found in parts of plants that when eaten passes through the body but is not completely digested; it helps food move through one's intestines and is important for good health

grate (GRATE) to reduce to shreds by rubbing against something rough

low-fat (loh-FAT) food that has three or fewer grams of fat per serving

mash (MASH) to crush or pound into a soft mixture

nutrients (NOO-tree-uhnts) things that are found in food and are needed by people and animals to stay healthy

organic (or-GAN-ik) grown without using chemical fertilizers or pesticides

preheat (PREE-heet) to turn on an oven and allow it to heat up to a specific temperature before using

pre-made (PREE-mayd) already prepared

preservatives (pri-ZUR-vuh-tivz) chemicals put into foods to keep them from spoiling

produce (proh-DOOSS) fruits and vegetables

protein (PROH-teen) a substance that helps one keep strong and healthy, and is found in meat, cheese, eggs, and fish

pureed (pyoo-RAYD) to make a smooth, creamy substance out of crushed fruit or vegetables

rind (RIND) the tough outer skin of certain fruit

simmer (SIM-ur) to boil slowly at a low temperature

sodium (SOH-dee-uhm) a chemical found in salt that the body needs in small amounts; too much salt in one's diet can cause health problems

steam (STEEM) to cook food by heating it in steam from boiling water

vitamins (VYE-tuh-minz) substances in food that are necessary for good health

Index

Bibliography

Chef AJ with Glen Merzer. *Unprocessed: How to Achieve Vibrant Health and Your Ideal Weight*. Charleston, SC: Kale Publishing (2011).

Shaw, Maura D. and Sydna Altschuler Byrne. *Foods from Mother Earth: A Basic Cookbook for Young Vegetarians (And Anybody Else)*. Wappingers Falls, NY: The Shawangunk Press (1994).

Read More

Carle, Megan and Jill, with Judi Carle. *Teens Cook Dessert*. Berkeley, CA: Ten Speed Press (2006).

West, Robin, Robert L. Wolfe, and Diane Wolfe. *My Very Own Mother's Day: A Book of Cooking and Crafts*. Minneapolis, MN: Carolrhoda Books, Inc. (1996).

Learn More Online

To learn more about making spring treats, visit
www.bearportpublishing.com/YummyTummyRecipes-Seasons

About the Author

Marilyn LaPenta has been a teacher for more than 25 years and has published numerous works for teachers and students. She has always enjoyed cooking with her students and her three children, and looks forward to cooking with her three grandchildren. Marilyn lives in Brightwaters, NY.